THEN & NOW

HUNTINGTON

THEN & NOW

HUNTINGTON

Terry L. Baldridge

ISBN 978-0-7385-6667-2

Library of Congress Control Number: 2009932286

Published by Arcadia Publishing
Charleston SC, Chicago IL, Portsmouth NH, San Francisco CA

Printed in the United States of America

For all general information contact Arcadia Publishing at:
Telephone 843-853-2070
Fax 843-853-0044
E-mail sales@arcadiapublishing.com
For customer service and orders:
Toll-Free 1-888-313-2665

Visit us on the Internet at www.arcadiapublishing.com

On the Front Cover: The Frederick Hotel Building, photographed around 1930 from the northeast corner of Fourth Avenue and Eleventh Street, has changed little when compared to a photograph from today. From the American Bank and Trust Company to fashion stores, establishments have come and gone as generations of shoppers frequent downtown Huntington's business district. (Then photograph courtesy of the James E. Marrow Library, Marshall University.)

On the Back Cover: Pictured in the 1930s are the Cabell County Courthouse Clock Tower and Huntington City Hall. (Photograph courtesy of the James E. Marrow Library Archives.)

Contents

ACKNOWLEDGMENTS

I would like to thank my favorite Huntington native, my dear son and friend, Keenan MacLean Baldridge. He patiently accompanied me as I researched and photographed the city on many warm and humid days in the summer of 2009. Many thanks to Marshall University and the James E. Marrow Library; the Cabell County libraries in West Huntington, Guyandotte, and Barboursville; the Frederick Building; Huntington City Hall; the St. James Building; the Guarantee National Bank Building; the Boyd County Public Library in Ashland, Kentucky; James Powers; WSAZ-TV 3; the *Herald Dispatch*; the Greenup County Public Library; Canon USA; the *Ashland Daily Independent*; the VA Medical Center; Melissa Adkins; the West Virginia Building; Pullman Square; City of Barboursville; the *Greenup News Times*; WUGO/WGOH; Allen and Brown; Red Lobster; my friends at the Kingdom Hall; and my very patient wife, Heather.

Introduction

For as long as many can remember, Huntington, West Virginia, has severed as a travel touchstone to the West or to the East via the Ohio River or railroad. Beginning with a collection of log cabins and huts near Guyandotte to the present, Huntington continues to grow and look forward with anticipation.

The area was first explored by Capt. Celeron de Bienville and his group of explorers in 1749. Nearly 30 years later, the area was granted as payment of veterans of the French and Indian War. The area changed hands over the years, and eventually the land between the Big Sandy River to the west and the Guyandotte River to the east caught the eye of Collis P. Huntington and his Chesapeake and Ohio Railway around 1869. In 1871, the city was chartered and named for Huntington.

Today within Huntington are scenes and structures that have changed little over time. They serve as touchstones or links with generations that have gone before us. Perhaps we will preserve some of them as a link from us to tomorrow.

CHAPTER 1

Huntington from Above

Some changes to Huntington's cityscape are quite notable on a close inspection of this aerial photograph from the early 1940s above Chesapeake, Ohio. The two-lane Sixth Street Bridge was replaced in the early 1990s with the four-lane Ninth Street Bridge. (Then photograph courtesy of the James E. Marrow Library Archives.)

The older photograph from the early 1930s was taken by Thomas Studios from the rooftop of the Chaffin Building. The familiar Cabell County Courthouse Clock Tower and Huntington City Hall have changed little. The courthouse has been extended and a gold covering added to the cover of the clock tower, the original east and west wings. (Then photograph courtesy of the James E. Marrow Library Archives.)

The photograph above is looking north toward downtown Chesapeake, Ohio, to where the Sixth Street and Ninth Street Bridges will come to rest. This photograph was taken around 1915 and was 17 years before the area's largest flood, therefore there is no flood wall in it. The ferry between West Virginia and Ohio can be seen almost center of the picture. (Then photograph courtesy of the James E. Marrow Library Archives.)

This photograph is looking from central Huntington toward the eastern part of the city and the small block of Marshall College in the upper left hand corner. Fourth Avenue disappears behind the building as the top of several prominent structures stand proudly in both photographs going north and south. Huntington has many beautiful and varied architectural styles that appeal to the eye. (Then photograph courtesy of the James E. Marrow Library Archives.)

Looking east between Fourth and Fifth Avenues, the older photograph dates from 1915 and shows a lone streetcar running between Seventh and Sixth Streets. Located in the same area today on Fourth Avenue and Sixth Street is the Department of Veterans Affairs Regional Office. Note the size of the trees surrounding the stately looking Cabell County Courthouse in the older photograph; they appear to be not more than saplings. (Then photograph courtesy of the James E. Marrow Library Archives.)

A couple of horse-drawn wagons move along snow-covered Tenth Street around 1915. A large "Use Alpha Flour" advertisement is on the south side of the old six-story mill. To the right, where Red Lobster is located today, is the three-story Mountain State Factory building. Pullman Square is shown in the modern photograph on the left. (Then photograph courtesy of the James E. Marrow Library Archives.)

The hill layout of Ohio has changed very little when comparing the now photograph with a picture taken in 1915. The classical front of the Masonic Building on Third Avenue can easily be picked out in both photographs. Just behind the Masonic Building is the coal temple extending over the Ohio River with its track extending east. (Then photograph courtesy of the James E. Marrow Library Archives.)

The Island Creek Coal Temple extends out beyond the Huntington side of the Ohio River. Coal mined in West Virginia's hills and mountains made its way to Huntington via the railroad; here it was unloaded onto barges where the coal made its way to various factories throughout the United States. Today the site is the location of a boat dock and Harris Riverfront Park. (Then postcard courtesy of the James C. Powers collection.)

The older photograph shows Huntington from the hills above Ritter Park around 1920. Note how sparse the neighborhood is between Eighth Street and Ninth Street and how small the trees are in Ritter Park. The recent photograph was taken from the Guarantee Bank Building looking south along Eighth Street toward the hills above the park. Much has changed throughout the years when viewing Huntington from above. (Then photograph courtesy of the James E. Marrow Library Archives.)

Looking north on Ninth Street as Huntington's largest building, the West Virginia Building, reaches several times higher than any structure in this photograph from 1950. When constructed in 1924, the building began as the Union Bank and Trust Building. In the 1940s, it was renamed and was the original home to the area's first television station, WSAZ. (Then photograph courtesy of the Cabell County Public Library.)

CHAPTER 2

Scenes and Structures

Constructed in 1927 and 1928, the Keith-Albee Theater was just one of over 150 vaudeville theaters around the world to be financed and built by vaudeville investors B. F. Keith and Edward Albee. When the theater opened in early May 1928, it was the second-largest theater in the United States. New York's Roxy Theater was the largest. (Then photograph courtesy of the James E. Marrow Library Archives.)

Photographed on a cold January day in 1906 is the construction of the old post office and courthouse on the southwest corner of Fifth Avenue and Ninth Street. As two women pose in front of the unfinished building, what appears to be two stone masons can been seen working more than two stories up. Today the front of the building has changed little over 103 years. (Then photograph courtesy of the James E. Marrow Library Archives.)

This photograph of the old U.S. Post Office and courthouse dates from around 1948. Very little of the face of the structure has changed over the years. The most significant changes are the vehicles. Notice the Guaranty Bank and Trust building in the background of both photographs. This beautiful building has been a companion to the federal courthouse for many decades. (Then photograph courtesy of the James E. Marrow Library Archives.)

The older picture postcard shows the back of the post office and courthouse from Fifth Avenue and Eighth Street. The postcard view is from around 1910 and shows the federal building before the noticeable expansion of the classical structure. Several homes were purchased and dismantled in order to proceed to where the building is today. (Then photograph courtesy of the James C. Powers Collection.)

The Orpheum Theater hosted many vaudeville acts before the era of motion pictures. This photograph from around 1920 shows the Orpheum Theater during its heyday with the original St. James Building in the background. The St. James Building was constructed in 1914 and expanded to its present state in 1925. The theater is now the cinema on Fourth Avenue. (Then photograph courtesy of the James E. Marrow Library Archives.)

This old picture postcard dates from the early 1900s and is looking east of Fifth Avenue from near Eighth Street. Many of the residence buildings pictured during this time have been replaced with businesses, banks, and a library. There are many beautiful and historic structures along Fifth Avenue including the old Carnegie Library Building, which opened in 1904. (Then postcard courtesy of the James C. Powers Collection.)

The now photograph shows the growth over the years along Third Avenue from Ninth Street. Pullman Square, which includes a bookstore, shops, restaurants, and a state-of-the-art movie theater, has become a major draw for Huntington. Note in the postcard from the early 1900s that many businesses called this small portion of Huntington home. (Then postcard courtesy of the James C. Powers Collection.)

Huntington's city hall stands unmovable like the Parthenon in this photograph from around 1930. This structure has many classical elements, such as the column entrances on Fifth Avenue and Eighth Street. The entrances are reminiscent of structures designed by a true classical student and third president, Thomas Jefferson. The upper-story windows have incorporated similar elements. (Then photograph courtesy of the James E. Marrow Library Archives.)

This photograph dates from around 1930 and shows the old Anderson and Newcomb Company Building, also known as the Stone and Thomas Department Store Building. The six-story building was constructed back in 1904 and served as a department store from that time until 2000. The building is located on the south side of Third Avenue between Ninth and Tenth Streets. (Then photograph courtesy of the James E. Marrow Library Archives.)

A crowd of worried onlookers gathers at the intersection of Fourth Avenue and Ninth Street as the swollen Ohio River makes an unwanted visit to downtown Huntington. This picture dates from January 1937 and helps generations today see how extensive this great flood was. The best source of information as well as photographs can be found in James Casto's *The Great Ohio River Flood of 1937*. (Then photograph courtesy of the James E. Marrow Library Archives.)

This picture postcard from around 1912 shows the old six-story Thompson Building that was located on Ninth Street near the alley of Third and Fourth Avenues. The building served several generations of patients and clients as a doctor and lawyer's office. In the now photograph, a crane stands guard over the empty lot as if trying to capture the old charm of the long-forgotten building. (Then photograph courtesy of the James E. Marrow Library Archives.)

Built in 1874 and occupied for a time by economist and 1932 U.S. presidential candidate William "Coin" Harvey, this beautiful home on Third Avenue is a window to Huntington's post–Civil War past. The Enslow home is to the right of the W. H. "Coin" Harvey home in the older photograph dating from 1892. (Then photograph courtesy of the James E. Marrow Library Archives.)

Many Huntington businesses as well as homeowners suffered like never before because of the 1937 flood. This photograph from January 1937 demonstrates the magnitude of the devastation. The floodwaters reached between Fourth and Fifth Avenues. Note the man at the far left of the picture wading in water almost waist-deep near the base of the West Virginia Building. (Then photograph courtesy of the James E. Marrow Library Archives.)

The photograph above is from the late 1920s and is centered up the Huntington Dry Goods Company department store at Third Avenue and Ninth Street. The Thompson Building can be seen in the background to the left. To the right of the store was the Empire Loan Office and the Gold Furniture Company. Today the Marshall Hall of Fame Café is located in the old Dry Goods Company building. (Then photograph courtesy of the James E. Marrow Library Archives.)

This photograph was taken in 1932 by Thomas Studios from the first floor of the Frederick Building just across Fourth Avenue from the Keith-Albee Theater. The photographer was looking east at the intersection of Forth Avenue and Tenth Street at the base of the St. James Building to the right. The Coal Exchange Building towers in the background. (Then photograph courtesy of the James E. Marrow Library Archives.)

Designed by Verus T. Ritter and constructed during World War I on Eighth Street, Huntington High School was a considered a state-of-the-art school for its time. Like he had done when designing Huntington's city hall, Ritter incorporated the classic column look for the main entrance. The structure would house high school students faithfully until 1996. (Then photograph courtesy of the Cabell County Public Library.)

To ease the effects of student overflow, a second magnificent structure was constructed on Huntington's east end in 1939 and 1940. Located on Fifth Avenue, Huntington East High School served teenagers on that side of Huntington for nearly 56 years when both Huntington High and Huntington East merged to form the Huntington High School Highlanders. (Then photograph courtesy of the Cabell County Public Library.)

Opening in 1956, Cabell Huntington Hospital has expanded to meet the needs of patients throughout Huntington and the area. Many changes are noted when comparing today's photograph with that taken not long after opening. The 313-bed hospital specializes in burn, neonatal, and pediatric intensive care as well as serving as a teaching hospital affiliated with Marshall University's School of Medicine. (Then photograph courtesy of the James E. Marrow Library Archives.)

In 1924, St. Mary's Medical Center began its unfailing commitment to the tristate when it accepted its very first patient. Today the area's largest hospital is an employer to nearly 2,600 people and has an inpatient capacity of over 390 beds. The photograph shows the hospital about five years after being constructed in 1930. (Then photograph courtesy of the James E. Marrow Library Archives.)

Photographed around 1929 is the old Huntington's Children's Hospital with five children posing at the entrance. Unlike anything in the area during this time, this hospital specialized in taking care of ill children with just over a dozen inpatient beds. Today the location is home to the Huntington Federal Savings Bank on Fifth Avenue. (Then photograph courtesy of the James E. Marrow Library Archives.)

Constructed in 1931 and 1932, this private building has served as a residence for doctors, nurses, and their families at the Veterans Affairs Medical Center. Pictured is building eight, which is located on the southern ridge of the medical center campus along with four similar structures. Today these structures are undergoing a major renovation in order to care for the needs of veteran patients. (Then photograph courtesy of Material Management and Steve Boyes.)

Many residents of Huntington over the years have become accustomed to the sound of trains traveling along the tracks. To an outsider, the sound of steel wheels rubbing against the steel track can be a major distraction, but after living near the tracks for some time, people hardly notice it. Pictured are an engine running through Huntington around 1950 and the wonderful Baldwin Engine 1308 on display near Ritter Park on Fourteenth Street West. (Then photograph courtesy of the Collis P. Huntington Railroad Historical Society.)

The Chesapeake and Ohio (C&O) Railroad station was one of the first structures many would see when arriving in Huntington. The building is still an impressive structure along the tracks near the Huntington downtown fire department and the police headquarters. Located on the front lawn of the building is a statue of Huntington founder Collis P. Huntington. (Then photograph courtesy of the James E. Marrow Library Archives.)

Photographed from around 1895 is the Huntington Baltimore and Ohio (B&O) passenger station, which was built in 1892 by the Ohio River Railroad. Today the area is known locally as Heritage Station, which includes the Huntington National Bank, which may have been robbed by Jesse James. On display is the Elk River Coal and Lumber No. 10 locomotive, which has been parked in its location since 1977. (Then photograph courtesy of the James E. Marrow Library Archives.)

The Ensign Manufacturing Company's car works, foundries, and steam forge are pictured in the photograph from November 1889. The Huntington area has been a supplier of various sorts to the C&O Railroad, the B&O Railroad, and many short line railroads that operated locally. Today CSX has a locomotive shop in nearly the same location as the old foundry. (Then photograph courtesy of the James E. Marrow Library Archives.)

Huntington, as well as many communities along the Ohio River, was caught off guard in 1913 as the river rose to historic flood levels. Photographed during this time is Marshall College's Old Main building surrounded by the damaging cold waters. This photograph was taken from near where Sixteenth Street begins on Third Avenue. (Then photograph courtesy of the James E. Marrow Library Archives.)

In 1887, the Cabell County seat was moved from Barboursville to Huntington and the building of a new courthouse was planned. The site selected was near the center of town on a rectangular block between Fourth and Fifth Avenues, and plans were drawn up. The postcard photograph dates from around 1905 and shows a smaller courthouse than is known today. (Then postcard courtesy of James Powers Collection.)

This photograph is from around 1890 and shows the first city hall, which contained the fire and police departments and the mayor's office. Many area city halls had the same setup and not only took care of city business but also took care of the horses housed below. The structure was located on Ninth Street between Fourth and Fifth Avenues. (Then photograph courtesy of the James E. Marrow Library Archives.)

3 CHAPTER

PEOPLE ON THE STREET

There are scores of photographs with people conducting personal matters and business on Huntington streets. This photograph from 1888 shows several Hauck family members posing in front of their wallpaper store, which was located on Third Avenue near Eleventh Street. (Then photograph courtesy of the James E. Marrow Library Archives.)

Many in Huntington turned out to hear Theodore "Teddy" Roosevelt speak from the south side of the Cabell County Courthouse around 1901. Roosevelt traveled the area on railroad and boat to trump up support, often giving speeches from the train at the depot. Today the south side of the courthouse is quiet of such activity except for vehicles traveling along Fifth Avenue. (Then photograph courtesy of the James E. Marrow Library Archives.)

In this photograph, dating from around 1920, the circus comes to Huntington. It shows the decorated wagons and many teams of horses pulling clowns, performers, and animals. Many people pull over to watch the parade pass by their vehicles parked along Third Avenue. Notice the *Herald Dispatch* newspaper at its first location across the street and to the left. (Then photograph courtesy of the James E. Marrow Library Archives.)

A local band marches to the beat of drums west on Fourth Avenue just past the Ninth Street intersection as much of Huntington looks on during the 1964 Band Festival. Note that WSAZ-TV 3 is capturing the moment with cameras on the ground and just above the crowd. Bands from across Southern Ohio, Eastern Kentucky, and Western West Virginia would prepare weeks in advance to participate in events such as this. (Then photograph courtesy of WSAZ-TV 3.)

Fans fill Marshall College's Fairfield Stadium on the new stadium's dedication day, October 1928. The stadium would receive upgrades from time to time, such as additional seating and playing surface changes. Marshall won this dedication day game over Fairmont State Teachers College 27-0. Today the Thundering Herd plays in the spacious and updated Joan C. Edwards Stadium. (Then photograph courtesy of the James E. Marrow Library Archives.)

The 1895 photograph shows a number of men and women standing on the east side of the D. E. Abbott Company. Today visitors can explore the J. Taylor Auto Museum that is located in the same building in Old Central City on Washington Avenue. Note that the sign from the older photograph is still visible today. (Then photograph courtesy of the Cabell County Public Library.)

Pictured is the Aleshire Harvey Company, a real estate business, with a Dr. J. H. Steenbergen occupying the second floor of the small structure. Today Huntington has many local, small businesses throughout the city that have become fixtures in the community. The current photograph shows one of the favorite antique shops, Hattie and Nan's, in Old Central City. (Then photograph courtesy of the James E. Marrow Library Archives.)

The photograph from around 1930 shows an automobile dealership that specializes in selling Fords and serves part-time as a service station. Huntington has seen many auto dealerships come and go throughout the last 90 years. Dutch Miller, which is located on Huntington's West Side and in Barboursville, has been a steadfast business in the area since 1961. (Then photograph courtesy of the James E. Marrow Library Archives.)

Shown in this image from 1931 are several businesses between Tenth and Eleventh Streets on Fourth Avenue: J. L. Cook Hardware Company, Kearney's Sporting Goods, and the Strand. Today, looking west from near the same location, several Huntington landmarks can be viewed: the St. James, the Keith Albee Theater, the Frederick Building, and the West Virginia Building towering in the background. (Then photograph courtesy of the James E. Marrow Library Archives.)

Like many older communities in the United States, Huntington has seen specialty stores and shops succumb to larger national chain stores. The Flournoy Hardware Company pictured in 1927 is displaying push mowers and a wheelbarrow on the sidewalk. The city of Huntington is working to bring back the days of small businesses, hopefully in the near future. (Then photograph courtesy of the James E. Marrow Library Archives.)

Proud bricklayers and engineers stand atop a smokestack in this photograph taken where Fifth Avenue would eventually run. The workers constructed the stacks for the Ultramarine and Color Company in the 1920s. Today the railroad track location is being used, and the area is now home to Flint Group Pigments, Turnpike Ford, and Stewart's Original Hot Dogs. (Then photograph courtesy of the James E. Marrow Library Archives.)

The old Cavendish Brothers department store supplied everything that a home would need. Notice the fine china in the shop window. Like the Cavendish brothers in the 1930s, there are still several dedicated, family-owned businesses that operate in Huntington. Gibbs Retail Systems, for instance, located on Bridge Street in Guyandotte, has been taking care of local customers since 1969. (Then photograph courtesy of the James E. Marrow Library Archives.)

The photograph from 1933 is of Montgomery Ward and Company and the Capitol Clothing Store. The Pullman Square center in downtown Huntington has brought in a number of restaurants, retail stores, and cinemas with marquees. The area sat dormant for several decades until 2004 when construction began on the north end of the property known as the "superblock." (Then photograph courtesy of the James E. Marrow Library Archives.)

The Lawrence Drug Store corner was an area of great activity, as the photograph from the 1940s captured. Nearby were the bus depot, Gold Furniture, and a café for lunch or a beer. Today the Big Sandy Super Store Arena attracts people throughout the area when it brings in many top entertainment acts, shows, and functions. (Then photograph courtesy of the James E. Marrow Library Archives.)

The photograph below dates from late 1935 and is of the Willard Service Station, Storage, and Batteries that stood at Fourth Avenue and Eleventh Street. It was a AAA-approved garage that would wash, grease, and repair automobiles in addition to selling gas and batteries. Today a parking lot occupies the old space where this building once stood. (Then photograph courtesy of the James E. Marrow Library Archives.)

A lone man travels north on Ninth Street around 1895 with the beautiful four-story Hotel Adelphi standing in the background. The building stood at the southeast corner of Ninth Street and Sixth Avenue. It was built in 1893 and sadly only lasted until July 2, 1901, when a fire destroyed the structure. This rare photograph was a gift to Marshall University from Mrs. S. S. McNeer. (Then photograph courtesy of the James E. Marrow Library Archives.)

This photograph from 1913 shows the magnitude of the flood that devastated many Ohio River communities. Here the Ohio River visits the Frederick Building at the corner of Tenth Street and Fourth Avenue. Today it is very hard to imagine that the river, which is quite a distance away, once flooded to this point and beyond in 1937. (Then photograph courtesy of the James E. Marrow Library Archives.)

Several businesses pictured tried in the vain to keep out the swollen Ohio River with boards nailed to the entranceways. Perhaps they wanted to keep out trespassers or keep debris from breaking their windows. Huntington today is surrounded by a flood wall that was constructed not too many years after the 1937 flood. There are also several dams that help to tame the river. (Then photograph courtesy of the James E. Marrow Library Archives.)

Pullman Square has brought in many businesses and jobs to the downtown Huntington area. This revitalization was quite a contrast from how employers and employees felt after the flood of 1937. The photograph shows the Community Savings and Loan Company, Piggly Wiggly, and the Capitol Market Company cleaning ruined furnishings and interiors. (Then photograph courtesy of the James E. Marrow Library Archives.)

"Where Third Avenue crosses Ninth Street," reads the sign on the east and north faces of the Huntington Dry Goods Store in early 1937. The sidewalks and streets are lined with debris that had been ruined by the muddy Ohio River. Today the scene is much different as patrons enter the Marshall Hall of Fame Café to dine. (Then photograph courtesy of the James E. Marrow Library Archives.)

Two firemen pose for the camera at the St. Cloud Station No. 4 around 1910. The structure was in use as a station until very recently. Today the building is still owned by the city of Huntington and used by the Department of Traffic Engineering. The old St. Cloud Station No. 4 is located in Central City just off Madison Avenue. (Then photograph courtesy of the James E. Marrow Library Archives.)

Six firemen stand ready for business in this rare photograph of Huntington's fire department Victor Hose Company No. 3. The men were ready day and night, as they are today, as evident by the lantern on the wagon. Today Huntington's finest are prepared to assist the city's inhabitants as indicated by the open doors of each engine garage. (Then photograph courtesy of the James E. Marrow Library Archives.)

Back in 1890, the mail was delivered by horse and buggy, railroad, and steamboat. Various companies competed and the most economical or lowest offers were awarded contracts to deliver the mail. In this photograph is the U.S. Mail Packet *Chesapeake* stopping to deliver and receive mail and goods near Huntington. (Then photograph courtesy of the James E. Marrow Library Archives.)

Pictured is a trim boat, the *Nancy*, built in 1894 at Huntington. Today the Ohio River is busy with activity both day and night. Photographed a couple of decades ago, part of Ashland Oil's fleet of barges that delivered coal and oil products included the *Ashland*, *Paul Blazer*, and *Tri-State* just to mention a few. (Then photograph courtesy of the James E. Marrow Library Archives.)

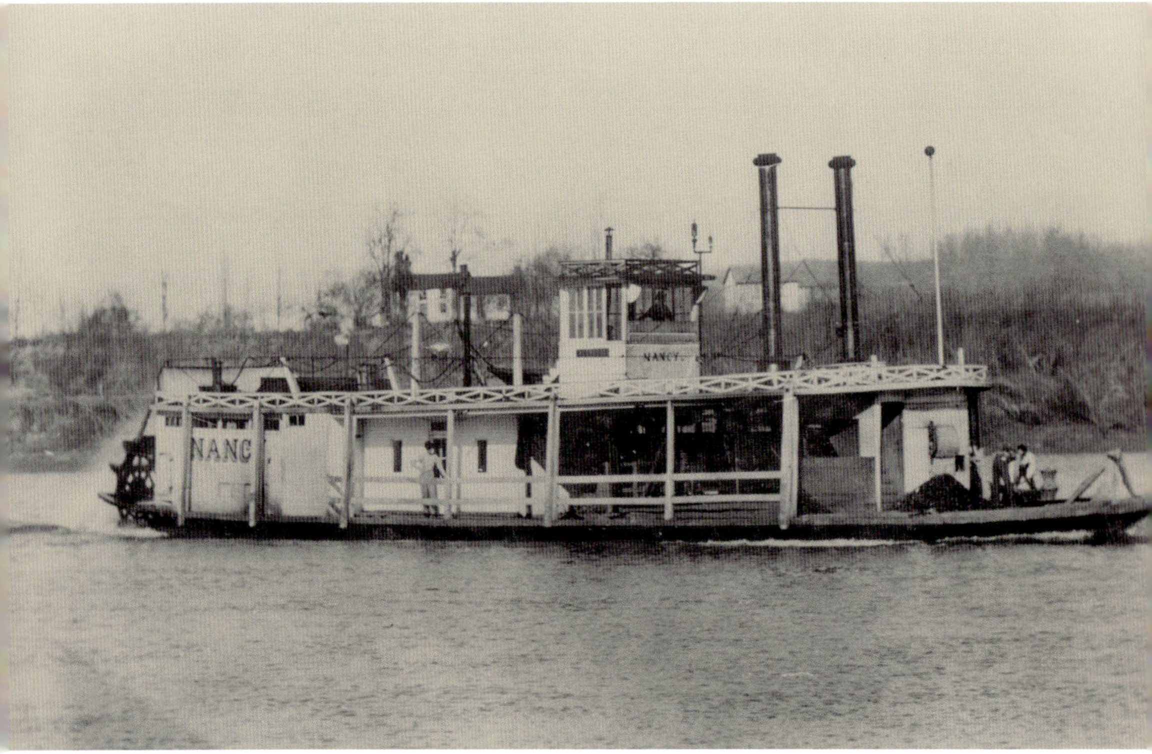

Most assuredly the horse to the far right will be looking for work as the motorized taxis become more popular for quicker travel. This photograph is from around 1925 and shows the eight taxicabs and one horse that belonged to the tristate's largest taxicab company, the Huntington Taxicab Company, with its three-digit phone number. (Then photograph courtesy of the James E. Marrow Library Archives.)

With the use of open flame and electric wire that wasn't isolated, the threat of fire was a constant concern for many. This 1905 picture shows the shell of the Barlow Henderson Wholesale Dry Goods Store that stood on the northeast corner of Third Avenue and Eleventh Street. Note that the three young men are not wearing shoes. (Then photograph courtesy of the James E. Marrow Library Archives.)

Pictured from the late 1880s is a muddy Huntington street filled with horses, wagons, and many area farmers buying and selling. Sadly, farms are not as plentiful as they once were in the area; however, Huntington and the Pullman Square section attract shoppers eager for a good deal or a great meal. The square has parking garages and street parking to meet the needs of all visitors. (Then photograph courtesy of the James E. Marrow Library Archives.)

Swimmers in 1925 take to a small boat dock on the Ohio River on a hot and humid summer day. The location is near Twenty-sixth Street and just across the river near where Chesapeake and Proctorville come together. Today swimming is prohibited in these areas because barges being docked cause strong down currents, which are very dangerous. (Then photograph courtesy of the James E. Marrow Library Archives.)

The boat ferries two cars and, no doubt, several passengers to Huntington as the Sixth Street Bridge is being completed in the background. The bridge would last from the late 1920s to 1994 when it was demolished and replaced with the Ninth Street Bridge or the Robert C. Byrd Bridge, which opened to four lanes of traffic in 1994. (Then photograph courtesy of the James E. Marrow Library Archives.)

This photograph was taken of children attending model school at Marshall College in 1905. The clothing, transportation, and Sixteenth Street are quite different from today; however, Old Main looks now as it did then. The entrance and familiar architecture style of the buildings that make up Old Main face Huntington to the west. (Then photograph courtesy of the James E. Marrow Library Archives.)

Many students picnic on the south-side lawn of Old Main in 1904, as downtown Huntington is visible in the background to the east. Today the view shows very few residential buildings but mostly Sixteenth Street and Fourth Avenue filled with students on their way to one of the many near-campus restaurants to eat. (Then photograph courtesy of the James E. Marrow Library Archives.)

This appears to be a bricked Eight Street heading south toward the hills above the Ritter Park area. The tracks let the reader know that during the late 1920s, a person could choose to ride the trolley to the park, or from that area to downtown Huntington, or even to Ashland via Kenova and Catlettsburg. Today there are few signs left that trolleys ran on the streets throughout Huntington. (Then photograph courtesy of the James E. Marrow Library Archives.)

Pictured is Huntington's first electric trolley, which ran through Huntington to Guyandotte and back several times a day. It could remain on a schedule, whereas the road conditions made it difficult for other methods of transportation to get a person to a desired location on time. Notice the terrible shape of the streets in the 1880s in downtown Huntington. (Then photograph courtesy of the James E. Marrow Library Archives.)

People are dressed and ready to pick up a family, friend, or old acquaintance at the old C&O Railroad depot, which was right behind the newly constructed depot. At upper right one can see the brick chimney of the new depot in the background. Today there is nothing but tracks and railcars where the old depot once stood. (Then photograph courtesy of the James E. Marrow Library Archives.)

The new depot was an incorporation of classical Greek Revival and traditional doorways with a beautiful cover that kept passengers dry or in the shade on hot days. President Clinton kicked off his reelection bid here at this stately railroad station back in the mid-1990s. The area around the station was packed in order to hear him speak before he boarded the presidential campaign train. (Then photograph courtesy of the James E. Marrow Library Archives.)

If it were not the 1930s, one would assume that this was some sort of hat-wearing club of women, but during this time almost everyone wore a hat. These women are eager to begin shopping at Anderson Newcomb's 35th anniversary sale. The photograph was taken on Third Avenue across from the fountain at Pullman Square. (Then photograph courtesy of the James E. Marrow Library Archives.)

CHAPTER 4

ONE LAST GLANCE

Huntington's Fifth Avenue runs into Guyandotte and would have had to go over this Roebling-type suspension bridge that was built in the 1870s. The bridge lasted until the early 1900s when it was replaced completely by metal, making it long-lasting and strong. (Then photograph courtesy of the James E. Marrow Library Archives.)

The older image is the earliest known of the area, done by a French artist from the Proctorville, Ohio, side of the Ohio River back around 1819. Guyandotte was the scene of a Civil War battle that is reenacted every year on its streets. The recent photograph shows the beautiful Twenty-ninth Street Bridge looking over the river at Guyandotte. (Then photograph courtesy of the James E. Marrow Library Archives.)

As pictured on the banks of the Guyandotte and Ohio Rivers, logs too numerous to count jam the smaller river as far as the eye can see in 1900. Lumber was harvested up the river, floated down to the Ohio River, and sorted by type. The wood would be made into large rafts and moved via sternwheelers to the mills. (Then photograph courtesy of the James E. Marrow Library Archives.)

A raft was made by dozens of logs and moved to an area where a boat would push it to mills along the Ohio River. This photograph demonstrates the great size of the raft, men maneuvering the raft, and a houseboat where the water monkeys, or log riders, stayed during their time off. Notice the homes to the left of the river. Today a flood wall protects Guyandotte from high water and obstructs the view of the river. (Then photograph courtesy of the James E. Marrow Library Archives.)

The Guyandotte Suspension Bridge is preserved in this photograph from around the 1890s. More rafts are in the river and several houseboats of the workers are seen parked under the bridge on the eastern side of the bank. Today the metal bridge, located on Fifth Avenue leading into Guyandotte, is closed to traffic. (Then photograph courtesy of the James E. Marrow Library Archives.)

The old tollhouse, built in 1837 on the banks of the Guyan River, was moved to its current location and restored in 1950. The person working in the tollhouse would collect tolls and transport travelers across the river. Today the house is located on Main Street in Barboursville and is part of a historic walking tour of homes and locations within the village. (Then photograph courtesy of the James E. Marrow Library Archives.)

Part of Barboursville's old Morris Harvey College, founded in 1888 as the Barboursville Seminary, is shown here. The buildings included separate dormitories for young men and women as well as education structures. Today the area is the location of the West Virginia Veteran's Home and the Nancy Cartmill Gardens and is a popular stop for weddings. (Then photograph courtesy of the Terry L. Baldridge Collection.)

Pictured is a postcard of the Barboursville Bank and Hotel Edgar between Center and Water Streets. The structure has been referred to as the Brady Hardware Building for many years. Today the building is home to several small businesses and is located across the street from the water fountain in the gardens. (Then photograph courtesy of the James E. Marrow Library Archives.)

Ashland, Kentucky, is considered part of the Huntington metropolitan area. Pictured is the 1922 construction of the Ashland National Bank Building. The building stands at a height of 116 feet and 11 stories and is currently the home of the Community Trust Bank. The structure has changed very little over the last 87 years. (Then photograph courtesy of the Boyd County Public Library.)

The Crump and Field Building on the northeast corner of Greenup Avenue and Fourteenth Street is a fine example of 1890 classical architecture. The older photograph shows the 1913 flood that destroyed many wooden structures along the Ohio River. Today many travel between Ashland and Huntington via Catlettsburg, Kenova, and Ceredo. (Then photograph courtesy of the James C. Powers Collection.)

Ashland photographed from an airplane in the late 1940s looks somewhat similar to its sister city Huntington, West Virginia. Many structures in both cities as well as in Ironton and Portsmouth, Ohio, were designed and constructed by the same architects and construction companies. Huntington has much to offer in the way of business and entertainment. (Then photograph courtesy of the James C. Powers Collection.)